George Jacob Holyoake

Manual of Co-Operation

Being an Epitome of Holyoake's History of Co-Operation

George Jacob Holyoake

Manual of Co-Operation
Being an Epitome of Holyoake's History of Co-Operation

ISBN/EAN: 9783337280925

Printed in Europe, USA, Canada, Australia, Japan

Cover: Foto ©Suzi / pixelio.de

More available books at **www.hansebooks.com**

MANUAL

OF

CO-OPERATION,

BEING

AN EPITOME OF HOLYOAKE'S "HISTORY
OF CO–OPERATION."

ARRANGED BY

THE SOCIOLOGIC SOCIETY OF AMERICA,

WITH AN INTRODUCTION

BY GEORGE JACOB HOLYOAKE.

———————

NEW YORK:
JOHN B. ALDEN, PUBLISHER.
1885.

CONTENTS.

MANUAL

OF

CO-OPERATION.

I.

ENGLISH CO–OPERATION IN 1885.

THOSE who have done me the honor to make writings of mine on Co-operation the basis of this epitome of the subject, ask me to make a brief Introduction to it, which shall bring the information in my History of the movement in England down to the present time. The authors of this work, (of which I write without having seen it,) have doubtless made a summary or selection of such portions or passages as have relevance to American needs, or as may be intelligible to the people of the United States. Of all that, they are the best judges. All that is required of me is, to make as clear as I can in a short paper, the English conception of the Co-operative movement, to-day.

Co-operation is organized self-help by honest labor and honest trade; the profits being equitably divided among those who create them, whether by work of hand or work of brain. That is what we understand Industrial Co-operation to be.

There is a familiar use of the word "Co-operation," which means two or more persons or things acting together to produce some result—as when a man and a lever act together to move a log, or a cat's paw is employed to pull chestnuts from the fire ; or when one thief holds the bag, while another thief fills it ; or as when a physician marries the daughter of an undertaker, with a view to unite the business.   In these cases, the log is not consulted, the cat gets no chestnuts; the owner is plundered by two thieves united, and the patient does not profit by the union of the pestle and the spade.   To the general public, these acts of concert equally mean co-operation.   We mean by the word, the Co-operation of honest Industry, with a view to an equitable share of the profits made.   We put the word "honest" into the definition because if the laborer and the trade be not honest, the public are cheated, and Co-operation is but an organized form of fraud.

Trouble has been taken by recent writers to estimate how far this new scheme of business has gained ground and advanced.   It is now generally admitted that eighteen years after the formation of the existing society of Rochdale Equitable Pioneers,—that is, in 1862—there were 450 stores established.   Ten years later—that is, in 1872—there were 920. In the next ten years—that is, in 1882— the stores had increased to 1200.

The number of members, which in 1862 were 90,000, had in 1872 increased to 340,000, and in 1882 they amounted to 640,000. The Share and Loan capital of the stores which was in 1862, £450,000, amounted in the next ten years to £3,340,000, and in 1882, it had reached £8,000,000.

The business of the stores rose also from period to period. The annual sales increased from £2,350,000 in 1862, to £13,000,000 in 1882. The profits made by the stores were not less remarkable. In 1862 they were £166,000. In 1872 £935,500; while in 1882 they had risen to £2,000,000.

The sum total of this co-operative activity is, that we now have about 1200 stores, or Distributive Societies, as we call them, which have 640,000 members, and £6,000,000 of share capital, and the annual sales of the Societies amount to £18,000,000.

All we have at present to show of workshop Co-operation are about twenty-two Producing, or Manufacturing Societies. These belong to the denomination of Farm or Workshop Societies. The aim of all is to establish the principle of Equitable Profit-sharing among working people. But there is not much done in this way yet.

There are also five Federal Corn Mills which grind corn for the stores in their districts. There are two Wholesale Societies—one in England and one in Scotland. The business done by the Manufacturing Societies is about £220,000; by the Corn Mills £1,300,000; by the Wholesale Societies £6,000,000. The annual business of all the societies exceeds £25,000,000.*

Distributive Co-operation is well established, and extending. Leeds, for instance, has upwards of 20,000 members. It has so many branch stores, and is so continually erecting new ones, that they keep a staff of builders who move from place to place as new stores have to be built. During the last twenty years the business done by working men is estimated at £250,000,000, and the profits about £20,000,000, all of which has gone into their own pockets. There are three Civil Service Stores in our Union, who do a business of £2,500,000; but as they are cheap selling stores their business is not included in the statistics given, which are confined to stores dividing profits in purchases. For the same reason Joint Stock Companies are not included among Co-operative Productive Societies because

* The latest facts of Co-operative progress, and the principles whence they have arisen, are presented in a new Manual entitled *Working Men Co-operators*, by A. N. DYKE ACLAND, M.A., of Oxford, and BENJAMIN JONES, one of the most experienced officers of the movement. Its ability of statement, fulness of detail, and wisdom of suggestion, constitute the book a sign and proof of co-operative progress.

the workmen do not participate in the
profits made.

Many stores have no Educational
Fund, but there is increase in this useful
respect.   No store that begins with one
ever goes back.   No store beginning
without it ever establishes one, not know-
ing that no investment pays like associa-
tive knowledge.

The two great Wholesale Buying Societies are more and more appreciated.
Without them, the stores cannot command genuine goods and commodities,
and cannot fulfil the first condition of a
store—that of guaranteeing pure, unadul-
terated articles.

There have lately been formed two
Societies for promoting Co-operative Production.   We value the extension of Co-
operation to the Workshop, because it in-
creases the means and the prospects of
labor, and therefore elevates it ; gives
labor a dignity—for self-dependence
and assured competence make dignity.
Every Co-operative Workshop in which
the worker receives his or her equitable
proportion of gain made, allures labor
and contents it.

Next to Co-operative Workshops—and
perhaps before them—is Profit—the sharing in factories and places of business
and commerce.   Manufacturers are increasing who offer their work-people a
participation in profits.   We hope before
long that Trades Unions will encourage

their members to prefer working for those firms in which Profit-sharing is adopted. One day workmen will refuse to work where this is not done.

State Socialism signifies State Patronage, which many are ready to administer at the public expense ; and many are willing to receive who despair of the better day, because despair has made them abject. When I first knew Rochdale, all the working people needed relief. All who could get it had it, and the chief hope of others was that the workhouse might not be too full when their turn came. Now they subscribe to relief-funds, to hospitals, present fountains to the town, and in all things give like gentlemen.

It is Co-operation which has enabled them to do this. It has transformed a similar class of people in a similar way in many towns. The fear of Ferdinand Lassalle that the working class must always be bound by the " brazen law of wages " and never have capital of their own, is no longer true, where Co-operation is adopted and persisted in. Many stores have now more money than they know what to do with profitably; it is therefore, that we are directing attention to investments in houses, farms, and manufactories. Thus it has been abundantly shown in England that Co-operation can permanently and definitely improve the condition of the people. It may accomplish this result slowly, but it accomplishes it faster than revolution would, and without sacrifice of life !

GEORGE JACOB HOLYOAKE.

34 *Alfred Place W.,*
 So. Kensington, London, S. W.,
   April 18, 1885.

II.

INDUSTRIAL CO-OPERATION: WHAT IT IS.

"CO-OPERATION means concert for the diffusion of wealth. It leaves nobody out who helps to produce it. It touches no man's fortune; it seeks no plunder; it causes no disturbance in society; it gives no trouble to statesmen; it enters into no secret associations; it needs no trades-union to protect its interest; it contemplates no violence; it subverts no order; it loses no dignity; it accepts no gift nor asks any favor; it keeps no terms with the idle, and it will break no faith with the industrious. It is neither mendicant, servile, nor offensive; it has its hand in no man's pocket, and does not mean that any hand shall remain long or comfortably in its own. It means self-help, self-dependence, and such share of the common competence as labor shall earn or thought can win. And this it intends to have, but by means which shall leave every other person an equal chance of the same good."—GEORGE JACOB HOLYOAKE.

"It seems to me desirable, no matter by what particular agency or mechanism it may be secured, that the men who give their labor to the concern shall to some extent share in the profit it makes. But in participation there are losses as well as gains; but the very fact that these occur will make the men who share in them understand and feel better than they ever did before, the responsibilities and difficulties of the employer; and if, as is quite possible, many having felt its difficulties, prefer the certainty of fixed wages, they at least have had their choice between the two systems. I am well aware that such a state of things as I have pointed out is one which cannot be brought about in a day. It is quite probable that there are some kinds of business in which it cannot be brought about at all; but it seems to me it is in that direction that the efforts of the best workers, and the ideas of the best thinkers, are tending; and we are not to be disheartened by a few failures, or disappointed because we do not at once hit on the best way of doing what has never been done before."—EARL DERBY.

"It is not Co-operation where a few persons join for the purpose of making a profit by which only a portion of them benefit. Co-operation is where the whole of the produce is divided. What is wanted is that the whole working class shall partake of the profits of labor. Of all the agencies which are at work to elevate those who labor with their hands, in physical condition, in social dignity, and in those moral and intellectual qualities on which both the others are ultimately dependent, there is none so promising as the present Co-operative movement. Though I foresaw, when it was only a project, its great advantages, its success has thus far exceeded my most sanguine expectations, and every year adds strength to my conviction of the salutary influence it is likely to exercise over the destinies of this and other countries."— JOHN STUART MILL.

" Co-operation is a scheme by which profits can be obtained by concert, and divided by consent, including with the producers the indigent consumer. The original and defensible purpose of Co-operation is the better distribution of wealth throughout the whole community, including the consumer. Co-operation to benefit the capitalist at the expense of the workman, or to benefit the workman at the expense of the consumer, still maintains a virtual conspiracy against the purchasing public. Such Co-operation leaves the third and larger class unprotected and unbenefited, save indirectly or temporarily."—GEORGE JACOB HOLYOAKE.

III.

CONDITION OF THE WORKING PEOPLE IN ENGLAND BEFORE CO-OPERATION BEGAN.

MATTERS were at a very bad pass in England with the working-people when Co-operation began. It is difficult in these times, when partial knowledge has mitigated the anger of misery, to estimate the intensity of that rage against the rich, which the ignorant and hungry felt, half a century ago. Men of free thought in religion, politics, or science, were treated as a criminal class. Common men were the vassals of the crown, the prey of the priests, the property of the tax-gatherer. The crown took their bodies, the mitre their souls, the state their means. They lived in ignorance, they labored without reward, and what is worse, many of them had no more sense than to put themselves like dry sticks, under the cauldron of corruption. The rise of machinery filled the working class with despair. The capitalist, able to use it, grew rich; the poor, displaced by it, were brought in great numbers to the poor-house.

A man so strong-thinking as Horace Greeley had his mind inclined to Protection by the misery he witnessed in his

father's household, when hand-loom weaving was superseded by merciless inven-
tions. The tendency of competition, in-
tensified by the introduction of machinery, lowered wages, and pushed the mass
of the workmen with increased force
against the walls of the workhouse. Mr.
Thompson, of Cork, commenced an address in 1826 to the distressed Spitalfields
weavers, thus:

"The system of labor by which your productive
powers have been hitherto misdirected is fast coming to its close. All kinds of labor, agricultural
and manufacturing, are rapidly approaching their
fated equality—the level of competition, or the
starvation price, the lowest that even in times of
average employment will support a miserable ex-
istence."

If one whom fortune had placed above
want, and education above prejudice, had
these impressions, no wonder the poor
desponded, and were generally confused.

At this time the workman naturally
fancied that the wealth which existed
through the instrumentality of his labor
and the use of capital, existed at his expense, and that he was poorer because
this wealth existed; that it had been
abstracted from his proper income, and
that if he did not work for the capitalist
he would be himself better off. But this
is not so. If the workman acted and
worked for himself alone, he would have
to do everything for himself and provide
everything for himself; would be, in fact,

a mere savage, without any food except what he could catch or fight for. And though the poor are kept down to the very limits of life and have to die early, they have conveniences and pleasures no savage can command.

It is by concert in industrial operations that wealth arises, rather than from individual isolated exertion. Since the workman is one of the instruments in creating the wealth, he ought to get a reasonable share of it. This he may obtain, not by taking it from those who have amassed it, which can only be done by fighting, bloodshed, and waste, and by setting a precedent which will expose him to similar attacks in his turn, but by employing the economy of Co-operation to save capital, or by entering into industrial partnerships to earn it. This has been the lesson taught by Co-operative thinkers alone.

2

IV.

HOW CO–OPERATION BEGAN.

ROBERT OWEN, of Newton, Montgmo-eryshire, Wales, afterwards of New La-nark on the Clyde, in Scotland, was first a draper's assistant, then a manager of cotton-mills at Manchester. He entered the employ of a Glasgow cotton-spinner, who had mills at New Lanark ; married his master's daughter, and became a part-ner in the business ; subsequently owner of it in conjunction with others.

In 1810 he opened what he called an Institution for the Formation of Charac-ter, containing commodious schoolrooms, one of them 90 by 40 feet, for the instruc-tion of children from infancy until they were educated. It was partly a benevo-lent, but mainly a well-considered, eco-nomic scheme. He wanted to see in his work-people more skill, better conduct, and an improved condition. To attain these ends he knew intelligence must be diffused among them. He acted on the principle that intelligence would prove a good investment. It did prove so. And thus it came to pass that education of members has always been deemed a part of the co-operative scheme among those who understood it.

The working people among whom
Robert Owen found himself were in ignorance, and vice, and discomfort. The
provisions made for the education and
welfare of their children have not been
excelled by those made for popular education by the most generous state in
America; and the weavers and their
wives knew that he who showed this more
than princely concern for their children
meant them well. They offered Mr. Owen
what he valued more than a baronetcy
—their confidence and co-operation—and
labor and capital worked together as they
had never worked before.

Thus the foundations of Co-operation
were laid by Mr. Owen and his associated
capitalists sharing with the laborers and
their families a portion of the common
gain; and the share falling to the employers was made greater than it could
otherwise have been, by the confidence
and co-operation of the working people.
In a letter of Mr. Owen to the *Times*
newspaper in 1834, he said, addressing
his early friend, then Lord Chancellor
Brougham:

"I believe it is known to Your Lordship that in
every point of view no experiment was ever so
successful as the one I conducted at New Lanark,
although it was commenced and continued in opposition to all the oldest and strongest prejudices
of mankind. For twenty-nine years we did without the necessity for magistrates or lawyers; without a single legal punishment; without any known
poor's-rate; without intemperance or religious ani-

mosities. We reduced the hours of labor, well-educated all the children from infancy, greatly improved the condition of the adults, paid interest of capital, and cleared upwards of £300,000 of profit."

As George Stephenson made railway locomotion possible, so Owen set men's minds on the track of Co-operation; and time and need, failure and gain, faith and thought, and the good-sense and devotion of multitudes have made it what it is. Robert Owen's heart was with that religion which, though weak in creeds and collects, rendered humanity service. No affluence corrupted him. While he saw gentlemen of his acquaintance adding thousands to thousands and acre to acre, and giving themselves up to the pride of family, of title, of position, he himself planned for the welfare of mechanics and laborers. He found no satisfaction in the splendor of courts so long as the hovel stood in sight. He felt as Mr. Bright, when he said:

" I do not care for military greatness or renown: I care for the condition of the people among whom I live. Crown, coronet, mitres, military displays, pomp of war, wide colonies, and a huge empire are, in my view, all trifles light as air, unless with them you can have a fair share of contentment, comfort, and happiness, among the great body of the people."

V.

SPREAD OF CO-OPERATION.

FROM 1820 to 1830 was what may be called the Enthusiastic Period, when the Co-operative principles grew in England, Scotland, and Ireland, in spite of much opposition and discouragement. Numerous periodicals were started, and many conferences held. Some notable rules were adopted by the various Co-operative Societies—instructive to this day, and worthy the attention of Co-operative Societies now. The following are some of them most desirable to note:

"Loans of capital to the Society, by its own members, shall bear an interest of £5 per £100, and are not returnable without six months' notice. . . . In the purchase and sale of goods credit shall neither be given or received. . . . Every member agrees to deal at the retail shop or store of the Society for those articles of daily use which are laid in of suitable quality, and sold at fair ready-money prices. . . . The name of any member who finds it inconvenient to deal to the amount of at least two shillings a week at this store, shall be laid before the Committee. . . . All disputes among members on the affairs of the Society are to be settled by arbitration. . . . Any member misbehaving may be expelled by vote of the majority of members at a quarterly meeting. . . . No husband shall be admitted a member without his wife's appearing before the Committee and ex-

pressing her consent. . . . A man is not eligible
to be a member unless he can read and write ;
and in general he must produce a specimen of his
work. . . . No member is eligible for this Committee until six months after admission to the
Society. . . . Members who shall be found to receive parochial aid without having made known
their wants to the Society, may be expelled at a
general meeting. . . . Every member engages to
subscribe weekly to a fund for the relief of sick
and distressed members, when called upon to do
so by the Society."

In 1830 there were 300 Societies spread
over England, Scotland, Wales, and Ireland.   A few Co-operators in Manchester,
in that year took 600 acres of waste land
upon Chat Moss, and contrived to culti-
vate it.   The first co-operative manufacturing community appeared in London,
during this year.

VI.

THE SOCIALISTIC PERIOD.

FROM 1831 to 1844, Co-operation has
to be traced through Socialism. Grand
schemes of life were revived, in which
idleness and vice, silliness and poverty,
were to cease by mutual arrangement.
This unattained, and hitherto unattain-
able, state of things, came to bear the
name of Socialism. Many congresses
were held, and numerous publications is-
sued, during this period.

VII

JOHN SCOTT VANDELEUR'S AGRICULT-
URAL EXPERIMENT.

In 1830, Mr. Vandeleur of Ralahine, Ireland, devoted 618 acres to the application of the Co-operative principle to agriculture. His tenantry were of the lowest order of Irish, poor, discontented, disorderly and vicious, and had been badly used. Yet, although he proposed to try his experiment under the most unfavorable state of society in the world, it is admitted on every side that it was a complete success. The government of the colony was absolute in Mr. Vandeleur, who retained the right of summary dismissal of any person brought upon the estate of whom he disapproved. Yet during the three years and a half the arrangement lasted (terminated only by his death), he never had occasion to use this summary power. The members of the community were elected by ballot among the peasants. The business of the farm was regulated by a Committee, also elected by ballot. The Committee assembled every evening, and assigned to each man his work for the following day. There was no inequality established among them. The domestic offices, usually per-

formed by servants, were assigned to the
members under seventeen years of age.

From this quiet community, established in the midst of terror and murder,
the landlord, Mr. Vandeleur, received
back in full all the money which he advanced for the wages of the laborers;
£200 a year interest on the working
capital; the stock, and farm implements,
and £700 a year rent. What induced the
laborers to work with such profitable
good-will was, that the members of all
ages above seventeen received an equal
share in the division of profits over the
above payments. Besides, a Co-operative
store was opened, similar to one at New
Lanark, where they obtained provisions
of good quality at nearly cost price.
Pure food, honest weight, and reduced
prices, filled them with astonishment.

Great care was also bestowed on the
education of their children. The school
was conducted on purely secular principles. Spirituous liquors and smoking
were prohibited on the estate. The Rev.
Francis Trench, brother of the Arch-
bishop of Dublin, visited the " New Systemites," as they were called, and wrote
out his approval of what he saw, in detail. The Society had made rules for
itself. One was, that no member should
be expected to perform " any service or
work but such as is agreeable to his or
her feelings." Irish human nature must
not be of bad material since both honest

and disagreeable work was daily done, and cheerfully. One day a mail-coach traveller found a man up to his middle in water, repairing a dam.

"Are you working by yourself?" inquired the traveller.—"Yes," was the answer.—"Where is your steward?"—"We have no steward."—"Who is your master?"—"We have no master. We are on a new system."—"Then who sent you to do this work?"—"The Committee."—"Who is the Committee?"—"Some of the members."—"What members do you mean?" asked the visitor.—"The ploughmen and laborers who are appointed by us as a Committee. I belong to the New Systemites." *C.*

When Mr. Craig, the Co-operative steward, first went among these men, who had shot the previous steward, they sent him a sketch of a skull and cross-bones, with an intimation that they intended to put him to bed under the "daisy quilt." As he went along the road, the people who did not know him, saluted him with the kind country greeting of "God be with you." One of his laborers told him that he should always reply in Irish "*Tharah-ma-dhœl.*" Accordingly, Mr. Craig answered everybody with this rejoinder; but observed that it did not make him popular. At length a friend explained to him that it meant "Go to the Devil!"

The man who taught this dangerous

answer became one of the best members of the Society; and once when the Co-operative steward was supposed to be lost in the woods he met "Tharah-ma-dhœl" looking for him. On being asked why he came out on that errand he answered: "We thought you lost on the Bog Mountain."—"Suppose I was lost, what then?" said the steward.—"Sure, sir," replied Tharah-ma-dhœl, "if we lost you, we should lose the System."

NOTE.—This experiment was subsequently given up, not owing to any defect in itself, but in consequence of his squandering his estate in other ways.

VIII.

CONSTRUCTIVE CO-OPERATION.

IT is of no consequence inquiring now
how it comes about, whether by fraud or
fate—the effect is the same—that the
great total of wealth, which capital and labor, thought and industry, have produced,
is found in possession of a few, and the
many run about anxious and precarious,
strongly advised to emigrate without de-
lay to some other land, where they find
that the same or a worse condition of
things prevails. Of two parties to one
undertaking, the smaller number—the
capitalists—are able to retain profits sufficient for affluence, while the larger number—the workers—receive a share hardly
sufficient to pay taxes; and by no parsi-
mony or self-denial can they secure for
themselves competence. No insurrection
can remedy the evil. No sooner shall the
bloody field be still, than the same principle of competitive struggling will repro-
duce the same inequalities, and the vic-
tors of to-day be plundered to-morrow
by those to whom they have taught this
murderous mode of redress.

A very different remedy has found favor
among industrial thinkers. By producers
giving security and interest for their own

capital, and dividing the profits earned among themselves alone, a new distribution of wealth is obtained, which accords to Capital equitable compensation and secures to Labor enduring provision.

Thus the advocates of the new form of industry, by concert, tried to induce society to combat competition by Co-operation, which promises to protect society from the further insurgency of individualism, by creating a field for its energy, and security for its reward. Instead of two men fighting which shall steal a field, which neither can honestly hold, Co-operators agree to buy it, to till it, and divide the produce. This is the species of constructive Co-operation whose origin and procedure is the new social feature of our time.

IX.

METHODS OF THE EQUITABLE PIONEERS.

THE men of Rochdale were they who first took the name of Equitable Pioneers. Their object was to establish Equity in Industry. Among them was an original, shrewd thinker, one Charles Howarth, who set to work to devise a plan by which capital could be obtained, and the permanent interest of the members secured. It was that the profits made by sales, should—instead of being taken by the few who were shareholders—be divided among all members who made purchases at the stores, in proportion to the amount they spent there; and that the shares of profits coming due to them should remain in the hands of the directors until it amounted to £5; and they should be registered as shareholders of that amount. This sum they would not have to pay in out of their pockets, for the good reason that they had not, and never were likely to have, the money. The store would thus save their shares for them; and they would thus become shareholders, without it costing them anything. So that if all went wrong they lost nothing; and if they stuck, like sensible men, to

the store, they might save in the same
way other £5, which they could draw out
as they pleased.

Thus by this obvious scheme (obvious
when once devised), the store ultimately
obtained £100 of capital from each twenty
members. For this capital they paid an
interest of 5 per cent. as an encouragement to members to adhere to the store
and save. Of course, before any store
could commence by which members could
make profits in this way, some of the
more enterprising promoters must subscribe some capital, in small sums or
otherwise, with which to obtain the first
stock. This was in Rochdale mostly
raised by weekly subscription of two-
pence. For every pound so subscribed,
an interest of 5 per cent. also was payable,
if the day of profit ever came. In order
that there might be as much profit as
possible to divide among purchasers, as a
means of attracting more members, interest was always kept down at 5 per cent.,
and hence 5 per cent. has come to be regarded as the Co-operative standard rate
of interest.

The merit of this scheme was that it
tended to create capital among men who
had none, and allured purchasers to the
store by the prospect of a quarterly divi-
dend of profits upon their outlay. Of
course, those who had the largest families
had the largest dealings; and it appeared
as though the more they ate the more

they saved—a fortunate illusion for the hungry little ones who abounded in Rochdale in those days.

The device of dividing profits with customers had occurred to others before it did to Mr. Howarth, though it was original with him. It had been seventeen years in operation at no very great distance from Rochdale ; and it might occur to the reader that Mr. Howarth may have heard of it. It is singular that it was not until twenty-six years after Mr. Howarth had devised his plan of 1844, that any one was aware that it was in operation in 1827.

Mr. William Nuttall, in compiling a statistical table for me, for insertion in *The Reasoner*, in 1870, discovered that an unknown Society at Meltham Mills, near Huddersfield, had existed for forty-three years, having been commenced in 1827, and had divided profits on purchases from the beginning. But it found neither imitators nor propagandists in England. Mr. Alexander Campbell also claimed to have recommended the same principle in an address which he drew up for the Co-operative Bakers of Glasgow, in 1822; that he fully explained it to the Co-operators of Cambuslang, who adopted it in 1831; and that a pamphlet containing what he said was widely circulated at the time.

Original ideas often occur to busy or cogitative minds. It is only when they occur to men of strong understandings, who discern their applications and advantages, and work out the mode of realizing them, that the merit of discovery is awarded.

From 1822 to 1844 stores limped along and failed to attract growing custom, while dividends were paid only on capital. During this time many minds must have been occupied in devising some method of increasing the interest of customers. To workmen unaccustomed to accounts, difficulties must have been felt in making out how books could be kept, recording purchases and dividing fractions of profit on small amounts. The solution proved simple enough eventually, and the process when devised, of giving metal checks, —introduced at Rochdale—representing the amount of purchases, which the buyer kept, made it simpler still. Then while the purchases were small, the trouble would appear greater than it was worth, and so long as dividends were trifling, the interest in the operation would be small. To explain the plan, to insist upon it, to devise its details, and carry them out during hopeless years of slow progress, was an affair of good sense, of strong sense, and human faith. And these were the merits of Mr. Howarth and the Rochdale Pioneers.

It was thus by taking the public into partnership that the revival of Co-operation came about. How slowly the first steps were taken on this new line of ad-

3

vance ; what patience, sagacity, and en-
thusiasm it required to increase the trav-
ellers upon it ; what prejudice law, religion, and ignorance put in the way ;
what moral improvement and pecuniary
benefit have resulted to hundreds of
thousands of families since, is already
matter of history.

The circumstances under which this
device was made, present some facts not
generally noticed, or not taken into ac-
count, if they are. When Mr. Howarth
made the proposal to divide profits among
purchasers it was the device of despair.
Stores, as has been related, had been argued down in some cases by impatient
Communists, and had gone down in others pretty much of their own accord.
Not a few had been aided in their descent
by a state of the law which favored the
development of rascally officers. Few
persons believed stores could be re-estab-
lished. When, therefore, on the revival,
customers at the store were scarce and
uncertain, so small a sum was likely to
arise to be given them—and for a long
time it was so small—that it proved
little attraction. The division of profits
among customers, though felt to be a
promising step, not being foreseen as a
great 'ortune, was readily agreed to. No
one foresaw what a prodigious amount it
would one day be. In 1876, the profits
of the Rochdale store amounted to £50,-

668, of the Halifax store to £19,820, and those of Leeds to £34,510.

Had these profits existed in Mr. Howarth's time, and had he proposed to give such amazing sums to mere customers, he would have been deemed mad, and not half-a-dozen persons would have listened to him outside the " theoretical " Co-operators. When twenty members constituted a Society, and they made with difficulty ten shillings a year profit altogether, the proposal to divide it excited no suspicion. A clear income of six pence a year, as the result of twelve months' active and daily attention to business, excited no jealousy. But had £40,000 been at the disposal of the Committee, that would have seemed a large fortune for forty directors; and no persuasive power on earth would have induced them to divide that among the customers.

Up to that time the shareholders in most places were merely multiplied shopkeepers, and they took all the profits. Had Rochdale directors of that day imagined what immense sums Co-operation would one day place at their disposal in that town, they would never have admitted the customer into partnership, nor carried out the proposal made. But when the proposal came in the form of dividing scanty and doubtful profits with scarce and reluctant customers, Mr. Howarth's scheme was adopted, and Co-operation rose from the grave in which ignorance, impotence, and short-sighted greed had buried it, and began the mighty and stalwart career with which we are now conversant. It really seems as though the best steps we take never would be taken, if we knew how wise and right they were.

At length the time came when substantial profits were made—palpable profits, actually paid over the counter, tangible in the pocket, and certain of recurrence, with increase, at every subsequent quarter-day. It took some years to attain them. But time was not counted when they did come. The fact was so unexpected that when it was generally divulged it had all the freshness and suddenness of a revelation to outsiders.

The effect of this patient and obscure success was diffused abroad; there needed no advertisement to spread it. When profits (a new name among work-people) were found to be really made, and known to be really had, by members, quarter by quarter, they were copiously heard of. The Co-operator, who had never had any encouragement from his neighbor, felt a natural pride in making him sensible that he was succeeding. As he had never had any success to boast of before, he was not likely to make little of this. Besides, his animated face suggested that his projects were answering with him. He appeared better fed, which was not likely to escape notice among hungry weavers. He was better dressed than formerly; which gave him distinction among his shabby comrades in the mill. The wife no longer had to " sell her petticoat," but had a new gown, and she was not likely to be silent about that. Nor was it likely to remain much in concealment. Her neighbors were not slow to notice her change in attire; and their very gossip became a sort of propagandism; and other husbands received hints that they might as well belong to the store. The children had cleaner faces, and new pinafores or jackets; and they propagated the source of their comfort in their little way; and other little ones communicated to their parents what they had seen.

Some old hen-coops were furbished up, and new pullets were observed in them; the cocks seemed to crow of Co-operation. Here and there a pig, known to belong to a co-operator, was seen to be fattening, and seemed to squeal in favor of the store. After awhile a piano-forte was reported to have been seen in a co-operative cottage, on which it was said the daughters played co-operative airs, the like of which had never been heard in that quarter. There were wild winds, but neither tall trees nor wild birds about Rochdale; yet the weavers' songs were not unlike those of the dusky toilers of the South, when emancipation first came to them :—

" We pray de Lord he gib us sign
    Dat one day we be free ;
De norf-wind tell it to de pine,
    De wild-duck to de sea.

" We tink it when de church-bell ring,
    We dream it in de dream ;
De rice-bird mean it when he sing,
    De eagle when he scream."

The objects of Nature vary, but the poetry of Freedom is everywhere the same. The store was talked about in the mills; it was canvassed in the weaving shed; the farm-laborer heard of it in the fields; the coal-miner carried the news down the pit; the blacksmith circulated the news at his forge; it was the gossip of the barber's chair—the courage of beards being then unknown. At public meetings, speakers arose with confidence quite new—that of men who had experience in possessing something, and something to tell of what their neighbors might do.

The "Toad Lane Store," as it was called, was the subject of conversation in the public-houses. It was discussed in the temperance coffee-shop. The landlord found his rent paid more regularly, and whispered the fact about. The shopkeeper told his neighbor that customers who had been in his debt for years had paid up their accounts. Members for the Borough became aware that some independent voters were springing up in connection with the Co-operative store. Pol-

iticians began to think there was something in it. Wandering lecturers visiting
the town found a better quality of audi-
tors to address, and were invited to
houses where tables were better spread
than formerly; and were taken to see the
Store, as one of the new objects of interest in town. A newsroom was opened
there, where more London newspapers
could be seen than in any coffee-house in
London ; and readers carried news of
what was being done in Rochdale, to
other towns.

News of it got into periodicals in London ; clergymen concerned for the social
welfare of the people heard of it; pro-
fessors and students of social philosophy
from abroad sent news of it home to
their country. And thus it spread far
and wide that the shrewd men of Rochdale were doing a notable thing in the
way of Co-operation. It was all true, and
honor will long be accorded them there-
for. For it is they, in whatever rank,
who act for the right when others are
still, who decide when others doubt, who
urge forward when others stand still, to
whom the glory of great change belongs.

The first we hear of Rochdale in Co-
operative literature is an announcement
in the *Co-operative Miscellany* for July,
1830, which " rejoices to hear,"

" Through the medium of the *Weekly Free
Press,* that a Co-operative Society has been formed
in this place, and is going on well. Three public

meetings have been held to discuss the principles. They have upwards of sixty members, and are anxious to supply flannels to the various Co-operative Societies. We understand the prices are from £1, 15s. a piece to £5, and that J. Greenhough, Wardleworth Brow, will give every information, if applied to."

At this very time the working people were in a desperate state. The Rochdale flannel-weavers had in June, 1830, a great meeting on Cronkey Straw Moor. There were as many as 7000 men out of employ; and there was an immense concourse of men, women and children on the moor, although a drizzling rain fell during the speeches. One speaker declared, "that wages had been so frequently reduced in Rochdale that a flannel-weaver could not, by all his exertions and patience, obtain more than from 4s. to 6d. per week." Mr. Renshaw, who spoke very well, said :

" That when his hearers went home they would find an empty pantry mocking their hungry appetites, the house despoiled of its furniture, an anxious wife with a highway paper or a King's taxes' paper in her hand, but no money to discharge such claim. God help the poor man when misfortune overtook him ! The rich man in his misfortune could obtain some comfort ; but the poor man had nothing to flee to. Cureless despondency was the condition to which he was reduced."

It was this year that the first Co-operative Society was formed in Rochdale. The meeting on the moor was in behalf of the flannel-weavers, who were then out on strike. The *United Trades Co-operative Journal* of Manchester recorded that notwithstanding the length of time the flannel-weavers and spinners had been out, and the slender means of support they had, they had contributed at two-pence per man, the sum of £30 as their first deposit to the Protection Fund ; and that one poor woman, a spinner, actually sold her petticoat to pay her subscription.

At the Birmingham Congress of 1832, the Rochdale Society sent a letter urging the utility of " discussing in Congress the establishment of a Co-operative Woollen Manufactory; as the Huddersfield cloth, Halifax, and Bradford stuffs, Leicester and Loughboro' stockings, and Rochdale flannels, required in several respects, similar machinery and processes of manufacture, they thought that Societies in these towns might unite, and manufacture with advantages not obtainable by separate establishments."

At that early period there were co-operators in Rochdale, giving their minds to federative projects. Their delegate was Mr. William Harrison, and their secretary Mr. T. Ladyman. Their credentials stated that " the Society was first formed in Oct., 1830, and bore the name of the Rochdale Friendly Society. Its members were fifty-two, the amount of its funds £108. It employed ten members and families. It manufactured flannel.

It had a library containing thirty-two volumes. It had no school, and never discussed the principles of Labor Exchange, and had two other Societies in the neighborhood."

It was deemed a defect in sagacity not to have inquired into the uses of Labor Exchanges as a means of Co-operative profit and propagandism. Rochdale from the beginning had a creditable regard for books and education, and "wholesale" combination was an early Rochdale idea. These and other facts of Rochdale industrial aspirations, prior to 1844, when the great Store began, show that this Co-operative idea was "in the air." It could hardly be said to be anywhere else until it descended in Toad Lane, and that is where it first touched the earth, took root and grew.

Of the "famous twenty-eight old pioneers" who founded the Store by their humble subscriptions of 2d. a week, only a few survive. Chief among the dead is James Smithies, its earliest Secretary, its ceaseless worker and counsellor. After a late committee-meeting in days of faltering fortunes at the Store or at the mill, he would go out at midnight and call up any one known to have money, and sympathy for the cause. When the disturbed sympathizer was awaked, and put his head out of the window, Smithies would call out: "I am come for thy brass, lad! We mun have it!"—"All right!"

would be the welcome reply ; and in one
case the bag was fetched with nearly
£100 in it, and the owner offered to drop
it through the window.—" No, I'll call in
the morning," Smithies replied with his
cheery voice, and then went home con-
tented that the evil day was averted.
In the presence of his vivacity no one
could despond: confronted by his buoy-
ant humor, no one could be angry.
There was such faith in his pleasantry,
that he laughed the Store out of despair
into prosperity.

X.

SUCCESS.

" WELL, after all," the unacquainted reader may exclaim, "what success was obtained, and by what arts was it won!" —By honest arts. Rochdale disowned artificial means of obtaining dividends. The Rochdale dividends have represented the simple, honest business profits of economy and good management. Look over the following page of facts reduced to figures.

Look at those columns of figures—they will bear scrutiny. They are not dull, prosaic, and statistical, as figures usually are. Every individual figure glows with a light unknown to chemists, and which has never illumined any town until our day. Our forefathers never saw it. They looked with longing and wistful eyes over the dark plains of industry, and no gleam of it appeared. The light they looked for was the light of material progress by the poor. Not a pale, flickering, uncertain light, but one self-created, self-fed, self-sustained, self-growing, and daily growing. Look, reader, at these figures again. Every numeral glitters with this new light. Every column is a pillar of fire in the night of industry. That is what common-sense and industrial cour-

Operations of the Society from 1844 to 1876.

Year.	Members.	Funds £.	Business £.	Profits £.
1844	28	28	—	—
1845	74	181	710	22
1846	80	252	1,146	80
1847	110	286	1,924	72
1848	149	397	2,276	117
1849	390	1,193	6,611	561
1850	600	2,289	13,179	880
1851	630	2,785	17,633	990
1852	680	3,471	16,352	1,206
1853	720	5,848	22,700	1,674
1854	900	7,172	33,364	1,763
1855	1,400	11,032	44,002	3,109
1856	1,600	12,920	63,197	3,921
1857	1,850	15,142	79,789	5,470
1858	1,950	18,160	74,680	6,284
1859	2,703	27,060	104,012	10,739
1860	3,450	37,710	152,063	15,906
1861	3,900	42,925	176,206	18,020
1862	3,501	38,465	141,074	17,564
1863	4,013	49,361	158,632	19,671
1864	4,747	62,105	174,937	22,717
1865	5,326	78,778	196,234	25,156
1866	6,246	99,989	249,122	31,931
1867	6,823	128,435	284,919	41,619
1868	6,731	123,233	290,900	37,459
1869	5,809	93,423	236,438	28,542
1870	5,560	80,291	223,021	25,209
1871	6,021	107,500	246,522	29,026
1872	6,444	132,912	267,577	33,640
1873	7,021	160,886	287,212	38,749
1874	7,639	192,814	298,888	40,679
1875	8,415	225,682	305,657	48,212
1876	8,892	254,000	305,190	50,668

age have done; that is what the generous watchfulness of a few gentlemen has promoted, and that is what the good sense of every reader will aid in rendering yet more triumphant—guiding other wanderers than Israelites out of the wilderness of helplessness, and far from the house of a worse than Egyptian bondage; because in these days there is none to deliver those who have not the sense to save themselves.

The Toad Lane Store has expanded into fourteen or more branches, with fourteen or more newsrooms. Each Branch is a ten times finer building than the original Store. The Toad Lane Parent Store has long been represented by a great Central Store, a commanding pile of buildings which it takes an hour to walk through, situated on the finest site in the town, and overlooking alike the Town Hall and Parish Church.

The Central Store contains a vast Library which has a permanent librarian, and the Store spends hundreds of pounds in bringing out a new catalogue as the increase of books needs it. Telescopes, field-glasses, microscopes innumerable, exist for the use of members. There are many large towns where gentlemen have no such newsrooms, abounding in daily papers, reviews, maps, and costly books of reference, as the working-class Co-operators of Rochdale possess. They sustain science-classes. They own property all over the borough. They have estates covered with streets of houses built for Co-operators. They have established a large corn-mill which was carried through misadventures, trying every form of industrial faith, by the energy and courage of Mr. Abram Greenwood. They contributed by experience and management, very largely to the creation of the great Wholesale Society of Manchester. They set the still greater example of instituting and maintaining to this day, an Educational Fund out of their profits. Theirs has been the chief propagandist store.

Their original objects were large. They sought to equalize the distribution of property; to create Co-operative workshops; to employ their own members, and support them on land of which they should be the owners, and create a self-supporting, intelligent, and prosperous community. They set out with high purpose, and therefore they have accomplished much.

Those who place before themselves lofty aims, ensure to themselves great modesty and great usefulness; whereas those whose aims are low, to them their littleness seems great; and they are proud, without having earned distinction.

XI

CO-OPERATION IN STORMY DAYS.

POLITICAL economists all predicted that Co-operation in days of adversity would fall into bad ways, and when the American civil war cut off the usual supply of cotton, those who regarded Co-operation as a "Great Eastern," too bulky for industrial navigation, naturally prophesied that it would founder in the Southern storm. The cotton scarcity, however, instead of destroying Co-operative Societies, brought out in a very conspicuous way the soundness of the commercial and moral principles on which they are founded.

Mr. Milner Gibson's Parliamentary Returns at that time, show that these Societies had increased to 454, and that this number were in full operation in England and Wales in the third year of the cotton-scarcity. The amount of business done by 381 of these societies was upwards of £2,600,000. In Lancashire there were 117 Societies, in Yorkshire 96. The number of members in 1863 in the 381 Societies was 108,000. The total amount of the assets of these Societies was £793,500, while the liabilities were only £229,000. The profits made by the 381 Societies (excluding 73 Societies which made no returns) were £213,600.

It may be safely concluded, therefore, that Co-operation established for itself a place among the commercial and social forces of the country. And the humble Co-operative weavers of Rochdale, by saving twopences when they had none to spare, and holding together when everybody else separated, until they had made their Store pay and grow great, set an example, and created for industry a new power, and for the working people a new future!

4

XII.

NATURE OF THE CO-OPERATIVE PRIN-
CIPLE.

WHEN Capital divides profits with
shareholders only, and as such, that is a
mere money-making affair. It is joint-
stockism. It is not a scheme that con-
cerns laborers much. It does not care
for them, except to use them. It does
not recognize them nor appeal to them,
nor command their sympathies, nor en-
list their zeal, or character, or skill, or
good-will, as voluntary influences and
forces of higher industry.

And, to do the joint-stock system justice, it does not ask for them. It bar-
gains for what it can get. It trusts to
compelling as much service as answers its
purpose. Even if by accident or arrangement, all the workmen are shareholders
in a joint-stock company, this does not
alter the principle. They are merely recognized as shareholders—or merely as
contributors of capital. As workmen,
and because of their work, they get nothing. They are still, as workmen, mere
instruments of Capital. As shareholders
they are more likely to promote the welfare of their Company than otherwise;
but they do it from interest, not from

honor ; they do it as a matter of business, rather than as a matter of principle. They are merely money-lenders ; they are not recognized as men having manhood. Joint-stock employers may have, and often do have, great regard for their men, and no doubt do more in many cases for their men than the men would have the sense to do for themselves. But all this comes in the form of a largess, a gift; as a charity, not as a right of labor ; not as an equitable proportion of earnings of profit made by the men. And the men, therefore, have not the dignity, the recognition, the distinction of self-provision which labor should possess.

If most workmen had a fund of capital, and could hold shares in all enterprises in which they were engaged in labor (quite an Utopian condition of society, not yet to be seen even dimly) they would be merely a capitalist class, regarding work not as a dignity or duty, or hardly so much an interest as a necessity. Their study would be how to get most by the employment of others; how early to desert work themselves, and subsist upon the needs of those less fortunate than themselves, to whom labor was still an ignominious obligation. What co-operation proposes is that workmen should combine to manufacture, and arrange to distribute profits among themselves and among all of their own order whom they employ. By establishing the right of Labor, as labor, to be counted as Capital—by dividing Profits on Labor—they would give dignity to Labor and make it honorable. They would appeal to the skill, good-will, to the utmost capacity and honest pride of a workman, and really have a claim upon him in these respects.

XIII.

CAPITAL.

ALL the nonsense talked about Capital, and the imputations heaped upon it, which political economists have so naturally resented, have arisen from workmen always seeing its claws, when it has mastery, absolute and uncontrolled. As the Master of industry, unless in generous hands, Capital bites very sharp. As the Servant of industry it is the friend of the workman. Capital is an assistant creator. It is nevertheless often selfish, and takes all the profits of the joint enterprise of money and labor. It can be cruel in its way; since it is capable of buying up land and abruptly turning people off it; it is capable of buying up markets and making the people pay what it pleases; it is capable of shutting the doors of labor until men are starved into working on its own terms. Capital is, like steam or fire, a good friend, but a bad master. As a servant it is a helper and co-operator. To limit its mastership it must be subjected to definite interest. Having received this, its claims are ended.

XIV.

PRODUCTIVE CO-OPERATION.

MR. ROSWELL FISHER, of Montreal, Canada, recognizes what I take to be the true theory of Productive Co-operation : *i.e.*, The Workmen should subscribe their own capital, or hire it at the rate at which it can be had in the money-market, at 5, 10, or 20 per cent., according to the risks of the business in which it is to be embarked ; then assign to managers, foremen, and workmen, of adequate experience and capacity, the minimum salaries they can command. Out of the gross earnings—wages—the hire of labor ; interest—the hire of capital; all materials, wear and tear, and expenses of all kinds, are defrayed.

The surplus is Profit ; and that profit is divided upon the labor according to its value. Thus, if the profits were 10 per cent., and the chief Director has £20 a week, and a skilful workman £2 the Director would take £100 of the profit, and the workman £10. The capital, whether owned by the workmen or others, would have received its agreed payment, and would have no claim upon the profits of labor.

XV.

DISTRIBUTIVE CO-OPERATION: THE CO-OPERATIVE STORE.

A MODERN Co-operative store generally commences and obtains success by five things:—

1. Intelligent discontent at being compelled to buy bad articles at a high price.

2. By opening a small, low-rented, clean shop, and selling good goods by honest measure, and at average prices.

3. Increasing the cheapness of goods bought, by concert of custom. The more money is taken into the market, the further it goes in purchasing; while the large custom gives full employment to the shopmen, and diminishes the relative cost of management.

4. By buying from wholesale dealers, the stock of the store can be obtained from the best markets, at the lowest rates, and of uniform good quality. It is by *continuity of quality*, that the prosperity of a store is established.

5. By capitalizing the first profits carried to the credit of the members, until they amount to $25 (£5). By this means, the first hundred members supply a capital of $2,500 (£500). Less than $25 to each member provides an insufficient capital.

In commencing a store, the first thing to do is for two or three persons to call a meeting of those likely to care for the object in view, and able to advance it. The callers of the meeting should be those who have clear notions of what they want to do, how it is to be done, and why it is attempted. Capital for the store is usually provided by each person putting down his or her name for a smaller or larger sum,—as each may be able—say from ten cents to twenty-five cents or more, per week—toward the payment of five shares of five dollars each. A small store may make a beginning with one hundred members who subscribe one share of five dollars each.

It is safest for members to subscribe their own capital: borrowed money is a dangerous thing to deal with. Interest has to be paid upon it, before any profits are made. By commencing upon the system of the intending co-operators subscribing their own capital, a larger number of members are obtained,—all have an equal and personal interest in the store, and give it their custom that their money may not be lost. This plan of dividing profits on purchases secures not only a common interest, but a large and permanent custom. It may take longer to collect the capital, but it lasts longer when it is collected, and is much more productive.

A secretary and a treasurer should be

appointed; and two or three nimble-footed, good-tempered, earnest fellows to act as collectors, who shall go round to the members, and bring into the treasury their various subscriptions. Some will pay their money unasked, but many must be solicited for their subscriptions. These collectors require to be men of infinite patience, and of practical sense. They are the real founders of the store, they cause the fund which creates it; they teach the first lessons of providence to hundreds of families, who else would never learn them.

Whatever business is entered into by the store, the members should get some intelligent, experienced man to put them in the right way of buying, and selling, and preserving stock. There are wholesale stores in England and Scotland, of which the smaller stores in those countries purchase. By means of this economical buying, first-class goods may be obtained at low prices. This is what Co-operation can give the members, and nothing save Co-operation can do this.

A true co-operator has three qualities; --good sense, good temper, and good will. Good sense—to dispose him to make the most of his means; good temper—to enable him to associate with others; and good will—to incline him to serve others, and be at trouble to serve them, and to go on serving them whether they are grateful or not in return, caring only that he does good, and finding it a sufficient reward to see that others are benefited through his unthanked exertions.

In a properly constituted Store, the funds are disposed of quarterly in seven ways :—1. Expenses of management.—2. Interest due on all loans.—3. An amount equivalent to 10 per cent. of the value of the fixed stock, set apart to cover its annual reduction in worth, owing to wear and tear.—4. Dividends on subscribed capital of the members.—5. Such sum as may be required for extension of business.—6. Say 2½ per cent. of the remaining profit. After all the above items are provided for, to be applied to educational purposes there remains:—7. The residue, and that only, is then divided among all the persons employed, and members of the Store, in proportion to the amount of their wages or of their respective purchases during the quarter.

At the Leicester Congress, 1877, thousands of copies of a clever little statement were circulated, which will suffice to explain to the most cursory reader what advantages a good Co-operative Store may confer upon a town :

1. It has made it possible for working-men to obtain pure food at fair market prices.—2. It has taught the advantage of cash payments over credit.—3. It has given men a knowledge of business which they could not otherwise have obtained.

—4. It has enabled them to carry on a trade of £160,000 a year.—5. It has made them joint proprietors of freehold property worth upwards of £20,000.—6. It secures them an annual net profit of £16,000.—7. It has raised many a man's wages two or three shillings a week without a strike! —8. It has alleviated more distress than any other social organization.

XVI.

THE CO-OPERATIVE WORKSHOP.

THE theory of a Co-operative Work-shop is very simple. Workmen who intend commencing one, first save, accumulate, or subscribe all the capital they can, as security to capitalists from whom they may need to borrow more, if their own is insufficient.

Nobody is very anxious to lend money to those who have none; and if any do lend it, they must seek a higher interest than otherwise they could think of, in consequence of the great risk of losing altogether what they lend. The workmen hire, or buy, or build their premises: engage or appoint managers, engineers, designers, architects, accountants, or whatever officers they require, at the ordinary salaries such persons can command in the market, according to their ability.

Every workman employed is paid wages in the same way. If they need capital in excess of their own, they borrow it at market rates, according to risks of the business—the capital subscribed by their own members being paid for at the same rate. Their rent, materials, salaries, wages, business outlays of all kinds, and

interest on capital, are the annual costs
of their undertaking. All gain beyond
that is Profit, which is divided among all
offices, and workmen, and customers, according to their salaries or services.
Thus in lucky years, when 20 per cent.
profit is made, a manager whose salary is
£500 gets £100 additional ; a workman
whose wages are £100 a year takes £20
profit, in addition to the interest paid
him for his proportion of capital in the
concern. There is no second division of
profit on capital ; the workers take all
surplus. And thus the highest exertions
of those who by labor of brain or hand
create the profit are secured, because
they reap all the advantage. This is the
distinctive principle of a Co-operative
Workshop.

Productive Societies have to go through
the same experience—more or less—
which befall Distributive Societies, before
they can acquire the wisdom or the confidence to adopt the policy of sharing
profits with the customer. Through not
doing this, many of these Societies have
peddled along a few years and ended in
bankruptcy ; or the affair has lapsed into
individual hands.

In the early history of Co-operation,
Productive Societies chiefly prevailed.
Few lasted and none flourished. They
fell, like the Distributive Stores, and for
the same reason : their customers had no
interest in continuing with them, stronger

than that which other manufacturers offered. When the revival of Co-operation came, and the Stores adopted the principle of sharing profits with purchasers, Productive Societies regarded its adoption by themselves (so far as they gave it any thought) as a mere " waste of profits." Yet it could be no less true that with yearly augmentation of custom, ever increasing capital would admit of a vast succession of manufactories being built; then an army of operatives being employed, and the great gains which come of great organizations being realized, profit would arise in the Workshop as in the Store.

Three things are necessary to production—labor, capital, and custom. Capital and Labor would have a poor time of it were it not for the Consumers who pay for their produce. Of these three, Custom alone is left idle. It supplies neither skill, means, nor attention. It is always away, and has to be sought, waited on, and often expensively looked after; while the Customer can be as active as any one if he has a motive. He can think, devise, point out what he wants, give orders, bring them, and procure them from others. In fact he can make it worth the while of any Producing Society to recognize him. It is quite time that Custom was put on duty and set to work.

The instinct of Co-operation is self-

help. Only men of independent spirit
are attracted by it. People have been
misled by the well intentioned but mis-
chievous lessons which have taught them
to depend upon mendicant supplication.
When the evil day comes ; when the parent has no means of supporting his
family or discharging his duty as a citizen,
the churches can render no help. The
State admits of no excuse; it accords
nothing but the contemptuous charity
of the poor-law. The day of self-help
has come; and this will be the complexion of the future. Co-operation, in im-
parting the power of self-help, abates
that distrust which has kept the people
down.

Above all projects of our day, Co-operative industry has eradicated the wholesale suspicion of riches and capitalists.
This means good understanding in the
future between those who have saved
money, and the many who need to save
it, and mean to save it.

War upon the rich is only lawful,
when, not content with their own good-
fortune, they close every door upon the
poor below them ; give no heed to their
just claims ; deny them—whether by law
or combination—fair means of self-help ;
discouraging the honest, industrious, and
thrifty, from ascending the same ladder
of prosperity on which they have
mounted.

Property has no rights in Equity, when

it owns no obligations of Justice, and ceases to be considerate to others. The power of commanding a pacifying distribution of means is afforded by the sagacity of Co-operation. As the power of self-existence in Nature includes all other attributes, so Self-help in the people includes all the conditions of progress. Co-operation is *organised Self-help.* That is what the complexion of the future must be.

XVII.

INDUSTRIAL PARTNERSHIP.—CONCLU-SION.

" It is human nature, I think, that a man should like to feel that he is to be a gainer by any extra industry that he may put forth, and that he should like to have some sense of proprietorship in the shop, or mill, or whatever it may be, in which he passes his days. And it is because the system— introduced of late years—of co-operative industry meets that natural wish, that I look forward with so much hopefulness to its extension. I believe it is the best, the surest remedy for that antagonism of labor and capital; for it is not in any way nec-essary to successful co-operation that the capital-ist be turned out of the concern."—EARL DERBY (then Lord Stanley) at opening of Liverpool Trades Hall, October, 1869.

AN Industrial Partnership is a business in which the employers pay to the hands a portion of the profits made, in addition to their wages, on the supposition that the men will create the said profit by an in-creased interest and assiduity in their work. In an industrial partnership capi-tal employs labor. In a co-operative workshop labor employs capital. The latter divides, not a share, but *all* the profits among the producers.

Mr. Owen, of Lanark, first showed mas-ters what they could, with profit, do by

5

acting on voluntary understanding of partnership with those they employed. But at this time the law of England forbade real partnerships between workmen and their masters, and his Industrial Equity was obliged to take the title of benevolence.—Industrial Partnerships owe to Fourier the principle of making labor a partner of capital, instead of merely its servant.

Mr. Charles Babbage, of England, argued that if some joint participation of profit in manufacturers was devised, the result of such arrangement would be :—

1. That every person engaged in it would have a direct feeling in its prosperity; since the effect of any success or interest off, would almost immediately produce a corresponding change in his own receipts.

2. Every person concerned in the factory would have an immediate interest in preventing any waste or mismanagement in all the departments.

3. The talent of all connected would be strongly directed to its improvement.

4. None but workmen of high character and qualifications could obtain admission into such establishments, because, when any new hands were required, it would be the common interest of all to admit only the most respectable and skilful; and it would be far less easy to impose upon a dozen workmen, than upon the proprietor of a factory.

5. And by no means least, that there would be removed, by common consent, the causes which compel men to combine for their own separate interests.

So that there would exist a union between employer and workman to overcome common difficulties, and promote a common interest. And such workman would be quite free to aid with his increased means, unions of fellow workmen elsewhere to attain similar advantages.

Industrial partnership is a policy of buying the skill and will of a man—his genius and self-respect, which elevates industry into a pursuit of art, and service into companionship. All this is a matter of bargain, not of sentiment. It is a scheme of reciprocity—not of benevolence on either side. An industrial partnership is but a better business arrangement.

But it is not well for co-operators to supplicate for these partnerships. They can make better ones by establishing workshops of their own. Better far to exact partnership terms, than to give an idea that charity is sought at the hands of employers. They can be obtained by combination. Trades Unions are the available means for this purpose. The working classes should assume a position where they neither supplicate nor depend upon the will of masters.

Co-operation has filled the air with new ideas of progress by concert. Men at first thought these to be mere flashes of light-

ning that play upon the fringe of the
tempest. They may better be compared
to the rainbow arch, which denotes a permanent truce between the waning ele-
ments, a sign that the storm is passing
away.

APPENDIX I.

A BIRD'S-EYE VIEW OF THE STORY OF CO-OPERATION IN THE UNITED STATES.

By R. Heber Newton, D.D.

1730 (*about*).—Share System introduced into New England Fisheries.

1752.—Fire Assurance introduced in Philadelphia. " The Philadelphia Contributionship for the Insurance of Houses from Loss by Fire;" Benj. Franklin first Director; corporation still prospering.

1767.—Life Insurance introduced in Philadelphia. " The Corporation for the relief of Widows and Children of Clergymen in the Communion of the Church of England in America;" composed of Clergymen; still flourishing.

1819.—Mutual Assurance bodied in a National Order—The Odd Fellows.

1820-30.—Owen's Movement; Socialistic.

1830-40.—Loan and Building Societies formed in Philadelphia.

New England Association of Farmers and Mechanics agitate the formation of Stores.

Labor organizations in New England open some Stores.

1840-50.—Brook Farm, Hopedale, etc.

Fourierite Phalanxes.

New England Protective Union builds up

a system of Stores; which at their height did a business of about $2,000,000 per annum; some of which still survive.

The earliest essay in Co-operative Production.

Tailors' Association in Boston (1849).

1850-60.—Loan Associations arise in Massachusetts.

Associate Dairies started in New York.

Anaheim.

1860-70.—Stores started in several States.

Productive Societies also.

Revival of Building and Loan Associations in Pennsylvania.

Mutual assurance assumes business forms.

Renewed attempts at co-operative production.

Ship-yard in Baltimore (1865), in Boston (1866); Machine Shop in Philadelphia (1866); Foundries in various cities, Shoe Manufactory in Lynn and in North Adams (*about* 1868), Cigar Manufactory in Westfield, Mass. (1869).

1870-80.—Knights of St. Crispin agitate Co-operation.

Founding and growth and decline of the Patrons of Husbandry; which order claimed to save in one year (1874) $12,-000,000 to its members, through its co-operative agencies.

Founding and growth of the Knights of Honor—a great Mutual Assurance Association still flourishing.

Founding, growth and dissolution of the . Sovereigns of Industry; which Order did a co-operative business in one year (1877) of $3,000,000, representing a saving to its members of $420,000; all of its Stores being on the Rochdale plan; some of which are still prosperous.

Scattered Stores in many States; Massachusetts reporting 15 independent Stores organized since 1870.

Philadelphia Industrial Co-operative Society, organized (1875).

Independent Productive Societies in many States.

Rapid growth of Associate Dairies, of which there are now 5000 in the United States.

Rapid growth of Mutual Assurance Companies ; the Patrons of Husbandry having at one time in one State alone 38 Fire Insurance Companies ; three Companies in one county carrying over $1,000,000 of risks ; New York State claiming 300,-000 members of various Mutual Assurance Societies at end of decade.

Rapid growth of Building and Loan Societies in Pennsylvania ; which now number over 600 in Philadelphia, with a membership of 75,000 and a capital of $80,000,-000 ; which number in Pennsylvania from 1500 to 1800 ; which have led to investment of $100,000,000 in real estate, in Philadelphia alone.

Revival of Loan Associations in Massachusetts ; where are now over 22 Societies incorporated, having a total membership of over 6000.

Institution of Loan Associations in New Jersey, Ohio, California, etc.; New Jersey reporting 106 Associations in 1880 ; Ohio reporting the incorporation of 307 Associations during the seven years preceding the report (1880) ; total estimated Societies (1880) 3000 in U. S., making membership of 450,000 and aggregate capital of $75,000,000.

Experiments in Colonization.

1880, *et seq.*—Formation of the New England Co-operative Association.

Revival of the Patrons of Husbandry.
Greatly quickened growth of Co-operation in all lines.
Development of the Knights of Labor.
Organization of the Central Labor Union.
Reports from all directions of new enterprises.

APPENDIX II.

THE SOCIOLOGIC SOCIETY OF AMERICA was organized in the City of New York May 24, 1882, when its Name, Constitution and By-Laws were adopted. It was founded by a group of women who had met to listen to a course of lectures upon Co-operation by Mrs. IMOGENE C. FALES, who has since served as the President of the Society. The membership is of both sexes.

The Society holds that the present industrial system, which regards labor merely as a Commodity to be obtained at the lowest market price, is unjust, and that the wealth derived from the joint action of capital and labor, is not equitably distributed. It believes that the measure of reward should be based upon the productiveness of labor, and not upon the law of demand and supply ; that competition—while it has produced good in the past, despite the suffering it has occasioned—is now reversing its action, and is working against the further progress of society ; that the nature of the principle, as it works itself out through an ad-

vancing civilization is to break down and
destroy weaker industries, and to concen-
trate wealth to such an extent as to dis-
turb the entire industrial system; and
that, in consequence of this, we are near-
ing a critical period where constructive
measures should be taken in order to
bring about a better social condition.

Those constructive measures are the
most rapid and thorough Organization of
Labor, industrial and political, with such
measures growing out of organization as
the necessities of the case may demand.
Also the introduction of the Rochdale
system of Distributive Co-operation, in
order to lessen the expense and increase
the means of living; Productive Co-operation, as a means to more closely unite
working men, diminish the number of
wage-earners, and give to those employed
the profit of their labor; Co-operative
Building Associations, in order that men
may own their houses, and that the
money now paid as rent may go toward
purchase.

The Society also holds that labor, as it
organizes, and becomes united in various
Unions, should recognize that those
Unions, while necessary as a means of
protection, are incapable of changing the
present condition of things and placing
Labor and Capital in harmonious rela-
tions. What is needed is, not so much
an advance in wages, as the concession of
the right of Labor to share in profits.

In other words, to introduce a new industrial system, where Capital is restricted to a fixed rate of interest, and Labor, over and above the market rate of wages, is allowed a share in the profits of the business.

This system of Industrial Partnership, or Co-operation, is precisely the reverse of our present one, which gives to Capital unrestrained and constantly increasing power, and holds to a stated but decreasing rate of wages, labor the great productive power of the world.

The work of the Society thus far has been carried on by such educational methods as could be commanded, such as lectures, parlor talks, and the publication and distribution of thousands of leaflets and pamphlets relating to Sociologic principles.

The central organization has now an extended membership with general officers and secretaries. Other local societies are in process of formation in addition to those of New York and Brooklyn.

IMOGENE C. FALES,
Pres. of Sociologic Society, Brooklyn, N. Y.

APPENDIX III.

WORKS UPON CO-OPERATION.

[The subjoined list of Works relating to the principles and working of Co-operation may be of use to those who wish to study the subject more thoroughly. The list is by no means complete, and many of the books are not easily accessible in this country, or perhaps in Great Britain.]

ACLAND, ARTHUR, H. D., and BENJ. JONES: Working-men Co-operators.

ARGYLL, DUKE OF: The Reign of Law.

BARNARD, CHARLES: Co-operation and Business.

BELLAMY, CHARLES J.: The Way Out.

BOLLES, ALBERT S.: Conflict between Labor and Capital.

DUNNING, T. J.: Trades Unions and Strikes. (Of this work John Stuart Mill says: "In it are treated questions of Trade Combinations, as seen from the point of view of the Working-man.")

ELY, RICHARD F.: Recent European Socialism.— French and German Socialism of Modern Times.—Christian Socialism in England.—German Co-operative Credit-Systems.—Labor and Socialism in the United States.—History of Political Economy in the United States.

GEORGE, HENRY: Progress and Poverty.

GRONLAND, LAURENCE: The Co-operative Commonwealth.

HARRISON, FREDERIC: Order and Progress.

HENNELL, MARY: Outlines of the Various Social Systems and Communities founded on Co-operation.

HOLYOAKE, GEORGE JACOB: History of Co-operation.—History of Co-operation in Halifax. —Self-Help: or History of the Equitable Pioneers of Rochdale.—The Logic of Co-operation. —The Policy of Co-operation.

HOWELL, GEORGE: The Conflicts of Labor and Capital (A History and Review of Trades Unions).

HUGHES, THOMAS: Trades Unions of England.

ICARIA: A Chapter in the History of Communism in the United States.

LAVELAYE, EMILE DE: Socialism of To-day.— Primitive Property.

LESLIE, T. E. CLIFFE: Essays on Political and Moral Science.

MILL, JOHN STUART: Principles of Political Economy.—On Liberty.—Chapters on Socialism.

MORRISON, WALTER: Village Co-operative Stores.

NEALE, ED. VAN SITTART, and THOMAS HUGHES: A Manual for Co-operators.

NEWTON, R. HEBER, D.D.: Co-operative Production in the United States.—Co-operative Distribution in the United States.

NORDHOFF, CHARLES: Communistic Societies of the United States.

PARE, WILLIAM: Ralahine Co-operative Farms.

PARIS, COMTE DE: Trades Unions of England.

PERIODICALS: The Co-operative News (Manchester, England).—The Present Day (London; edited by George Jacob Holyoake).—Building Association Journal (Philadelphia).—The Haverhill Laborer (Haverhill, Mass.).—John Swinton's Paper (New York).

RAE, JOHN: Contemporary Socialism.

REPORTS: Of Labor and Capital Investigations of the U. S. Senate Committee on Education and Labor (5 vols).—Of State Bureaus of Labor in Indiana, Illinois, Iowa, Maryland, Massachusetts, Missouri, New Jersey, New York, Pennsylvania, Ohio, Wisconsin.

ROGERS, HAROLD: Work and Wages.

ROSS, DENMAN W.: Early History of Land-holding among the Germans.

SMITH, ADAM: The Wealth of Nations.

SMITH, TOULMIN: History of the Early English Guilds.

SOCIOLOGIC TRACTS (*published by the Sociol. Soc. of Amer., who have also in preparation a book upon Social Economics*) : Social Evolution.—The New Civilization.—The Lower and Higher Laws of Nature.—Sociologic Principles, Nos. 1 and 2.

SPENCER, HERBERT: Principles of Sociology.

SYMES, DAVID: Outlines of an Industrial Science.

TAYLOR, SEDLEY: Profit-Sharing.

THORNTON, W. T.: Labor. ("In this work," says Mr. Holyoake, "the Philosophy of Union-ism and Co-operation are dealt with, with a completeness and impartiality not found else-where.")

VALLEVOREX, P. HUBERT: Les Associations' Co-operatives en France et à l'Etranger.

WARD, LESTER F.: Dynamic Sociology.

WATTS, J.: Co-operative Societies.

www.ingramcontent.com/pod-product-compliance
Lightning Source LLC
Chambersburg PA
CBHW021523270326
41930CB00008B/1063